T0114767

The
Thin
Place

A Special Place to Feel
the Presence of God

C.M. Williamson

WESTBOW
P R E S S®
A DIVISION OF THOMAS NELSON
& ZONDERVAN

WestBow Press books may be ordered through booksellers or by contacting:

WestBow Press
A Division of Thomas Nelson & Zondervan
1663 Liberty Drive
Bloomington, IN 47403
www.westbowpress.com
1 (866) 928-1240

Editor: Jessica Ingram

Scripture quotations marked KJV are taken from the King James Version.

Scripture quotations marked TLB are taken from The Living Bible, copyright © 1971 by Tyndale House Foundation. Used by permission of Tyndale House Publishers Inc., Carol Stream, Illinois 60188. All rights reserved. The Living Bible, TLB, and the The Living Bible logo are registered trademarks of Tyndale House Publishers.

ISBN: 978-1-6642-0035-7 (sc)
ISBN: 978-1-6642-0037-1 (hc)
ISBN: 978-1-6642-0036-4 (e)

Library of Congress Control Number: 2020913820

Print information available on the last page.

WestBow Press rev. date: 08/27/2020

For those who seek comfort and peace...

Contents

Acknowledgements

I am thankful and grateful to have been raised in a family dedicated to being a part of God's Church. I was raised in a family striving to learn more of God's Word. My family has been rooted in faith in God the Father and in the Holy Spirit living within us. Because of this, I have been fortunate to have known wonderful men and women of God.

I am grateful for the pastors, teachers, and church members who have strengthened my belief and understanding of God. Family, church members, teachers, and pastors have allowed themselves to be used by our gracious God to encourage my spiritual growth as a child of God.

I am deeply appreciative to a wonderful young lady who was an associate pastor in my church for the inspiration, guidance, and suggestions for this writing project. God used her to plant a seed in me.

Another wonderful pastor from my church successfully guided me through my first complete reading and study of the Bible. This generated in me a deep desire to read and study the Bible further.

I appreciate my friend who is a wonderful author. She provided encouragement, advice, and guidance from her experiences with writing. I truly thank you for the tools necessary for the completion of this book. I am so fortunate to have another friend who is a Sunday school teacher, an author, an educator, and an administrator. She provided much needed advice and information on publishing a book.

I am deeply thankful for my husband, Doug, and my daughter, who have been my greatest source of encouragement, believing in me always. These two never expressed any doubt that I would complete this task, although I was full of doubt. They constantly provide fulfillment to my life on this Earth.

Thank you to my mother, for the excitement shown and help given toward this book. God has richly blessed me with family and friends. I long for the days we will all be together once again in heaven with God.

Jessica Ingram has become a friend, an inspiration, a mentor, and a teacher. We found each other, not by chance, but by the grace and blessings of God. Jessica's faith in God is shown through her willingness to help. Thank you, Jessica, for being a servant of God. Thank you for your willingness to help me with this book. You are sincerely appreciated.

Also, I thank God for prodding me along to write. He showed patience with me when I found too many other things to do besides type. He provided the words and the confidence I needed to accomplish this task. I always stand amazed by guidance which God provides to me daily.

All glory to God!

C.M. Williamson

Preface

Have you ever had one of those experiences where you attended something or went somewhere with no particular intention or desire, but later realized God put you there? You may have heard something and just knew God intended for you to hear it. Well, one Sunday that happened to me. There was not anything different about that particular Sunday. This was not a special holiday on the church calendar. In fact, it was not out of the ordinary for God to speak to me through a sermon. God does that quite often. God knows that I am a person who has always needed to hear guidance or corrections in my life.

However, this particular time the pastor talked about the "thin places." She mentioned how we may have heard of them before — those places where heaven and earth come very close together. Those places where you know holiness is all around. Instantly, you feel no worry or concern. It is in those places of peace and comfort where you know without a doubt that you are not in control, but God is. You are reminded that the Holy Spirit is in you and around you. The angels are surrounding you.

Then it felt as if she was directly speaking to me. "You know, the thin place," she said.

I could not remember having heard of the "thin place" before, but I do understand the idea. So I got to thinking — that must be a place like the space between the boulders where God placed Moses, passed by him, and covered him with His hand to shield him. After passing Moses, God removed His hand and instructed Moses to look only at His back, not His face (Exodus 33:23 KJV). Certainly, a holy place was where Elijah went up by a "whirlwind" into heaven (2 Kings 2:11 KJV).

Heaven definitely came to earth in the place where Jesus Christ was born. According to the Gospels, it was such a holy place that God's angels filled the skies and sang praises. God even marked the birthplace with a star recognizable by others.

I think the "thin place" could be where John the Baptist took Jesus and baptized Him with water. At that very time, the Spirit of God came down like a dove. Then a voice from heaven told all who were there, in that place, that Jesus was His Son (Matthew 3:16–17 KJV).

It had to be a place like the Garden of Gethsemane, where Jesus prayed before he was arrested and crucified. The Gospels explain how Jesus talked with God the Father there. But perhaps the "thin place" is just any place where we might be. It could be any place where God the Father reaches down to hold us. In this place, He holds us closer than usual. Close, really close, to God!

I have been there! Not really realizing the miraculous place at the time, but it lives with me now. Now I see it because God the Father and His Son Jesus Christ opened my eyes. I needed to see it and remember it every day.

It is really hard to describe the "thin place" in the meager words of this world. I have experienced that moment of peace and comfort. That place where I am reminded that I need not worry for my God is in control. Good things or sad things may happen, but I need not worry.

A place where I not only know the Holy Spirit is with me and angels are helping me, but that place where heaven is almost on earth. It is the place where I can experience peace while on this earth right now. It is the place with God that I can never forget. You know, the "thin place." Praises to God! The "thin place!"

Although the memories I have of Daddy are my memories, I feel God planted a seed in my heart to share about my last week with Daddy.

The idea came not for the purpose of telling about my daddy, but to tell of the work of God, my Father in heaven.

So how should I put the events of the last week Daddy lived in a book? I certainly felt I had no words to put in a book. I have never even been an avid reader. How could I possibly do more than write a letter? I knew I had no experience in writing a book.

However, two very definite words came to me — **just type**! I even tried to dismiss the whole idea as one of my crazy thoughts. Dismissing the thought did not work. I tried to forget the command, but the words **just type** kept popping into my mind.

After several months, I gave in. I took my Bible, a few pages of handwritten notes, and sat down at the computer. Even with the tools I had gathered to assist me; I sat looking at a blank computer screen. What could I say? Then those very definite words came back to me — **just type**! How could I find the words? **Just type.** So, I started with a prayer each time I sat down to my computer, and I typed.

I do not consider myself a writer. I really have not even enjoyed reading a lot, except for my Bible. Therefore, I have no words to put in this book except to tell of my experiences with the Lord God. Even these words do not come from me, but from our Lord. I stand amazed and my soul shall ever sing praises to the Lord.

Therefore, these words are written to give glory to our Lord, to our God Almighty. These words are written for others to also see His glory. Feel the "thin place."

CHAPTER

Daddy

I miss my daddy….

I suppose many people say that all the time. All children miss their daddy when he is away. I miss Daddy, every day. Many others may also relate to this sense of loss. I lost Daddy to disease, but God reminds me that I have lost only Daddy's physical, earthly body. God provides me with this assurance.

Daddy always had a very distinct and wonderful scent about him. It was probably a men's cologne scent, but nevertheless, it belonged to Daddy. Since losing Daddy, I have still been able to smell that wonderful scent. Not only can I smell Daddy's presence, but occasionally an older man playing at the beach with his children or grandchildren will provide me with a glimpse of Daddy. I feel sure God is allowing me to experience precious time with Daddy once again.

He was Daddy to me, but to most other people, he was Cecil Gray McIntyre.

Daddy was strong, fearless, and patient. I could probably add to the list of words to describe Daddy indefinitely. In fact, I think the world would be a better place if all children could have a daddy like mine.

Of course, he was really only human, but I never thought of him as just a common, regular person. Daddy was strong and smart enough to do everything. He always, always protected us. Daddy could repair and build things without even reading the directions.

Although, I can remember times when Mama had to eventually pull out the directions, read them, and direct Daddy — of course he still had his own way of doing things. Yes, he was the smartest man around.

I feel sure that other people must have thought so as well because someone was always calling the house asking for him. Of course, that was during the time of house phones, and someone in the family would run to the phone to answer. The caller usually asked for Daddy.

The call would almost always be someone asking for advice or help. Daddy always had the most wonderful group of buddies who he would help; and they would help him in return. Although plenty others enjoyed Daddy's presence, best of all, he was and is my daddy!

Daddy worked hard to provide for our family. As a small child, I remember Daddy had his own air conditioning and refrigeration business. He usually went to work before I got up in the mornings. Then he returned home from work around dinner time or just before dark. We quickly learned that operating a business required a lot of time.

In my teenage years, Daddy worked for a company, but he continued to put in extra hours of work. So in the days he had off from work with his company job, Daddy worked in his shop repairing appliances to make a little extra money. His shop was actually just a three-car garage at our house, but it served as a terrific workspace for Daddy.

However, there was usually no space in the garage for actually parking cars. Daddy knew how to work on everything just a little bit and was a master at fixing many things. He was a Jack-of-all-trades, so to speak. He worked as an electrical supervisor at a large mill. Daddy was very smart at his work.

When something made funny noises or broke down, Daddy was a nice friend to have. And he always lent a helping hand. Daddy helped neighbors, his church, and served on every committee that had to deal with the church building or repairs.

All the people he helped were also willing to help him. It is nice when friendships work that way. Although he did have to work hard at the mill and at odd jobs for extra income, Daddy was ready to use his skills and knowledge to help friends and his church. Many times, Daddy worked just for the friendship. Yes, sir, he was a Jack-of-all-trades and a helper-of-all-people.

Although he worked hard and worked a lot, his family knew how important we were to Daddy. When Daddy had his own business, he oftentimes worked many hours, resulting in late nights.

In the late afternoons of the summer time, when my siblings and I were still young, we would run around in the front yard, singing to the top of our lungs.

We would sing things like, "Daddy, come ho-ome. We are ready to e-eat!" Then when Daddy did get home, we ate, talked, and played. Daddy always had time for us. Just as he was a dedicated worker, he was a dedicated father and he was good at that "job" as well. That particular job that day was playtime — and play we did.

I can remember Daddy chasing my sister and me around the house, sometimes even crawling on his hands and knees. Then we took off, running and giggling through the house. Daddy even knew how to dance with little girls standing on his feet.

Then, as we got older, Daddy knew how to make big girls feel better. On our many beach trips, Daddy's strong shoulders were perfect for standing on and jumping off of into the ocean water. Daddy would first kneel down, going under the water for us to step onto his shoulders. He would go all the way under so we could step up. Then he would catch us by the hands as he stood.

He rose out of the water and walked around looking for a good diving place for whoever was on top of his shoulders. It felt like being on the shoulders of a giant. He was a giant daddy diving board stomping slowly through the water — a motion which must have been similar to walking on the moon.

He would take time to play in the yard after a long day of work with my brother, passing the football and tackling each other. One or the other of them seemed to always get hurt, but then immediately would jump up and begin playing football again. Daddy would take time to watch bicycle maneuvers while working in his shop. During frightening times, Daddy was always the safety net.

Now, let me mention that I have a wonderful husband, Doug, who measures very, very close. But even today, Daddy is the smartest and bravest of all.

Daddy had a busy life before he had his family, as well. Like many men during the 1940s, Daddy felt the responsibility to serve his country at a very early age.

During WWII, the United States Maritime Service was allowed to enlist young men between the ages of 16 and 17 and one half years. This allowed the U.S. Maritime Service to train the young men for service in the Merchant Marines.

A requirement was that the application must contain the signature and approval of parents. Daddy's father would not agree, but his kind and loving mother, my Mama Mac, signed for Daddy to join.

It seems hard to imagine her doing such a thing. She must have done so, knowing he would not be happy doing anything else. But I know it was just the plan God had for Daddy. Mama Mac probably knew this as well. She was a kind woman and full of faith in God.

The U.S. War Shipping Administration posted that "young men can volunteer for a part in the winning of the war, before they reach the age of registration under the Selective Service."[1]

So, as Daddy would say he was off into adventures. However, according to Daddy, these adventures turned out to be unlike anything he could ever have imagined.

Like most veterans, Daddy did not talk a lot about war times and his experiences. He would tell of exciting adventures like helping to channel a ship through the Panama Canal.

Sometimes, the ships of the Merchant Marines would come under attack from the enemy in order to prevent them from delivering the supplies or the troops which were needed. Daddy could remember serving on fuel freighters and some of the dangers of guarding those ships from enemy attack.

In his occasional talks about his service in the Merchant Marines, Daddy admitted that everyone who had warned him was right — he really was a boy in a man's war.

But Daddy endured, faced his responsibilities, learned many lessons, and was glad to have served for the United States of America. God turned these war times into learning experiences for Daddy, providing experiences for him to become the person he was intended to be.

Later, Daddy was drafted to serve in the United States Army during the Korean War. (The Merchant Marines was not considered a branch of service at that time.) I do remember him telling me that some called it the "Korean Conflict." Daddy's response to that always was, "That was not a conflict, but a war."

As hard as this time may have been, Daddy seemed to have learned great lessons. God was at work.

After his war years and various jobs, Daddy settled down to start his own family. From then on, Daddy always had Mama by his side, supporting him in all he did. Daddy, Mama, and our grandparents, aunts, uncles, and cousins spoiled my siblings and me. Yes, we were loved and we knew it.

We had a wonderful Mamaw and Papaw and Mama Mac and Pop. We are still blessed to have a passel of aunts, uncles, and cousins.

I have many, many fond and treasured memories from growing up — similar to those which I have already mentioned. But one of my fondest memories is of one special family event that always took place on Sundays.

Every Sunday was a family church day for us. It was how my siblings and I were introduced to God. Sundays actually were very busy days.

The day began with Sunday school. Next, we went on to church worship together. We had lots of family at church too. Mama Mac and Pop, along with Daddy's sister, Aunt Norene, and her daughter Deborah would sit with us in church. We filled a whole pew. And that was without Mama. She sat in the choir loft since she was part of the choir. We didn't just fill one of the little side pews; we filled one of the long, middle section pews.

After church, Mama Mac almost always cooked Sunday lunch for everyone at her house. What a grand time it was! She actually cooked most of the meal before going to Sunday school. Now, as an adult myself, that is hard for me to wrap my mind around.

I now know that Mama Mac was very busy on Sundays. She must have had to get up early to prepare lunch and then make it to Sunday school. We were and have always been a family with God as our guide and protector, and the Word of God as our shield.

Now, I've mentioned a lot about me and Daddy, but I shared

Daddy with my big sister and little brother. We had a wonderful family — then and now. And we had wonderful childhood friends.

Life was enjoyed without thinking of what we had or did not have. It did not matter what someone else had; I do not even remember that being a thought at all.

As children, we never knew when Daddy and Mama were experiencing difficult times, although I have learned that tough times did occur. God warns us all that there will be trials, but He never leaves us. We were blessed with a God-centered family. God was and is with us.

Pardon me as I tarry off on this little bit of a rabbit trail for the purpose of briefly introducing Daddy. Again, I mention that I realize my Daddy to be only human, thus, I also know everyone may not hold him on the pedestal I do.

Certainly, he must have made his share of mistakes just like any human, but not in my mind. I know there is only one perfect Father, the Holy Father God of all the heavens, of earth, and of all creation. He is truly perfect.

I know He gave me Daddy, not by chance, but by plan. I will forever praise God for providing me with a wonderful, godly Daddy here on this earth. And now, I miss Daddy, but because of our Father in heaven, I know I will see him again. This provides unquestionable comfort. So I miss Daddy, fondly, daily.

But, this is not a story about me or my family or, really, even Daddy. It is a recollection of the wondrous plan of God the Father of all, since revealed. It is a story of His glory and grace, revealed. The heavenly Father, above all or anyone, watches over all of us and at all times. God is always caring for those who will trust in him. I am a living witness as to the plan God has always had for this family, but these words share just a glimpse of God's glory.

So, yes, I miss Daddy, but these words are to share an example of the marvelous works of God to His people — spending a week very close to God.

During this week, I was reminded the Holy Spirit is always with us. Oddly enough, it was a week of turbulence, yet comfort. It was a week of not really knowing what to do, but somehow things getting accomplished. A time where someone or something mystically carries everyone through the week, seemingly preplanned, yet, not planned by any of us.

So please be patient and forgive me when I digress, for I do so in order to better explain the events of this week. It was a week in the "thin place" where God and His heavens were very close. As always, the Lord God's Holy Spirit was with us. His angels were sent to administer to us. Always and forever He was and is with us; praise be to God!

Daddy in the United States Army after serving
in the United States Merchant Marines.

And thou shalt love the Lord thy God with all thy heart, and with all thy soul, and with all thy mind, and with all thy strength: this is the first commandment.

And the second is like, namely this, Thou shalt love thy neighbour as thyself. There is none other commandment greater than these. (Mark 12:30–31 KJV)

CHAPTER

I Believe

"When we walk with the Lord in the light of his
word, what a glory he sheds on our way![1]"

What beautiful, meaningful words from a hymn. These words are
so much a part of a real contented, happy life. How wonderful it is
to know that if we will walk with the Lord, guided by God's Word,
then the Lord is always with us. His Holy Spirit is among us and
within us. All we must do is believe in the Lord, ask the Lord, and
allow the Lord be a part of our lives.

The Lord God's promises are written in word to lead us. What
grace God the Father gives, always and forever! His Word, for life
everlasting, continues through years and years, further revealing
that our God's promises stand forever and ever.

So if we study God's Word and keep the Lord in our lives,
He will open our eyes to see His glory. Not only that, but He will
provide glorious lives for us here on His earth as well as with Him
in eternity. God warns of turmoil, but He sheds light for peace.

Trust in the Lord with all thine heart; and lean
not unto thine own understanding. In all thy ways

acknowledge him, and he shall direct thy paths.
(Proverbs 3:5—6 KJV)

How comforting! God's Word instructs us to trust and acknowledge Him, and He, the Lord, will direct a path for us. How easy life is supposed to be, according to the way God originally intended. Our Lord God wants us to acknowledge Him and believe, and He alone can give direction. He is the loving Father, wishing to be acknowledged because He is the Father, offering unconditional love.

Trust in the Lord and give Him the glory because He does such great and wonderful things for us. Because of our small thinking minds, it is hard to understand and even harder to totally trust, but God has a plan for all people. His plan is full of joy, peace, comfort, love, and kindness.

Yes, God has a glorious plan! We cannot accomplish such peace alone. What absolutely, wonderful, gracious love God has for us that He wants to provide so much.

What a wonderfully peaceful thought it is to be among God's angels, as well. I feel that we can walk among God's angels, perhaps not even realizing it at the time. Strength and comfort are felt, and peace is provided.

I believe this is because angels administer to us and the Holy Spirit is in us and among us. After Jesus Christ was crucified and resurrected, He visited with His disciples to explain the Holy Spirit.

And now I will send the Holy Spirit upon you, just as my Father promised. Don't begin telling others yet—stay here in the city until the Holy Spirit comes and fills you with power from heaven.
(Luke 24:49 TLB)

The Holy Spirit is promised and is with us, even now. The Spirit is not only promised, but promised from God the Father. The promise of the Holy Spirit for us was stated in word by Jesus Christ.

Wow, I have got it — I know, without a doubt, I am not alone in this world. I have got it! God knew and had a plan never to leave anyone alone on earth. Even though Jesus would have to be sacrificed and raised from the dead in order to save us, the Holy Spirit is here on earth to be with us, bringing power from heaven. I believe!

Not only does God provide His Holy Spirit, but I believe He sends His angels to administer to us. Every day I see miracles and feel the Holy Spirit with me. I wake in the mornings. I see and feel the warmth of the sunshine. I can speak and hear. I am a child of God and I am loved!

It is easy to take for granted the blessings of being healthy. What a blessing it is to be alive to help others. I am thankful that God opens my eyes to recognize the miracles He sends me every day.

Every day I recognize little mishaps that could have happened. Sometimes there are catastrophes which could have happened to me, but did not. It seems most evident in times when things would not go as usual or as planned.

One particular time while driving, I stopped at a busy intersection. I followed the driving rules just as I was supposed to do. The highway, which I was turning onto, was a very busy four-lane highway. I stopped, looked both ways, and then moved my foot off the brake toward the gas pedal. I moved my foot toward the gas pedal, but I could not touch the gas pedal. It was as if something was holding my foot.

I could not put my foot on the gas pedal. I even looked down to see if my foot was caught on something. The car would not go. What was happening?

Just as the whole idea registered in my mind, a car appeared on the highway — the highway I was about to turn onto. I had been protected from driving out in front of that car.

Satan was preparing for me to cause a vehicle accident, perhaps hurting others as well as myself, but God had a plan. Needless to say, I was a little shaken by the whole ordeal. The event happened in an instant, but time seemed to work in slow motion. I was in God's time. I was in the presence of angels. The Holy Spirit had taken over the entire situation. I was in that glorious moment — the "thin place." I was in a place where heaven came down. God and His angels were with me.

When focusing on God, our eyes can be spiritually opened to see and understand the Spirit with us and angels among us. Truly the Lord will direct our paths, and we are in the presence of holiness even on this earth.

Yes, I believe and declare that God is with me always. I believe He provides for all of us. However, I understand that each of us must be responsible for ourselves. I will always confess with my whole heart that I do believe in God the Father Almighty and that He is the maker of all things in heaven and on earth. I believe in Jesus Christ, God's Son. I know that the Holy Spirit is with me always, and that Jesus Christ has gone ahead to prepare a place for me in heaven.

What absolutely, positively wonderful peace it gives me to know that Jesus Christ is preparing for me. Not only is He preparing for me, but for all who acknowledge Him and believe on Him. How comforting to rest in the Lord, striving to live as He has shown us.

I know God is with me. I am a child of God's. I know that God the Father, His Son Jesus Christ, and His Holy Spirit walk with me.

I claim all blessings He has for me and my family. Praises be to God the Father that He does open my eyes so I can see His work. God is with me, especially in the "thin place!" I believe!

Daddy enjoying boating on a lake in Texas.

If you humble yourselves under the mighty hand of God, in his good time he will lift you up. Let him have all your worries and cares, for he is always thinking about you and watching everything that concerns you. (1 Peter 5:6—7 TLB)

3
CHAPTER

Struggles

God loves us. He loves us like a good Father, allowing us to make decisions. He created the Garden of Eden for us. God created it as a place for us to walk personally and daily with Him. He provided the perfect garden where everything was provided for us. God placed everything we would ever need in that garden.

However, mankind always struggles to trust God's plan. As a result, we chose a different path. This path allowed death, disease, and evil to enter the world. Mankind fell.

And even though God will always be with us, sending His Holy Spirit here on earth, adversity occurs. Therefore, troubles of this life strike, reality gives us a slap in the face, and tests in faith begin.

Just like anyone else, I experience struggles in this world. I do experience them, but not without the Holy Spirit by my side. I know and feel that I am always protected. But this was a particular struggle. It was a kind of struggle that I had heard about from others. But now, I was living through this struggle. Even so, the Lord was still on the path with me. God's glory provided light in the earthly darkness.

As terrible as tests of faith and turmoil in life can be, I now remember this struggle as a week-long walk in the glory and grace of God, because I believe.

I am assured the Lord is with me. His Holy Spirit not only took me by the hand and guided me, but picked me up and carried me when I could not move on my own.

His angels were sent to surround me. I felt assured that I was with Him. I felt the "thin place" where all that is Holy was with me. Praise to God that my eyes were opened to see and give God the glory!

I have mentioned I live in a family of believers. Our lives were always shaped by our Christian faith. I know the Lord God was alongside Daddy's earthly walk because of his faith.

Daddy lived such an interesting life here on this earth. He lived out his God-planned life.

Daddy grew up during the Great Depression; he served the United States in some of the great wars of this nation, and provided for our family. How could his life possibly not be interesting? Perhaps, not surprisingly, the last days of Daddy's life here on earth, were no less interesting.

Daddy became very ill from congestive heart failure which had taken over his body. In the last year, the disease restricted him a good bit.

Daddy was a person who liked to be outside. He enjoyed working on projects or doing odd jobs. Remember, after all, he was a Jack-of-all-trades.

After retiring — and by that I mean retiring from his full time electrical supervisor job and his part time air conditioning/ refrigeration business — Daddy started enjoying some of his hobbies. He enjoyed projects he never had time to do when he was working. I guess it was not really work, although sometimes the hobby projects turned into hard labor.

He decided to experiment with wood-building projects. I did not even realize Daddy enjoyed projects beyond electricity. I think Daddy just enjoyed a good challenge. Sometimes he may have even taken on a project just to see if he could do it.

He built some small projects such as blue bird houses. At times, he redesigned Martin bird houses. (Of course, a Martin house must be built in a specific way. If not made correctly, the bird will not choose to live in it.)

Daddy felt that he knew exactly what the Martin would like, so he created his own version of a Martin bird house. He also built a variety of bird feeders. But even the feeders had to be redesigned. Daddy had to build the feeder so squirrels could not steal the bird seed. I might add, not all of the Martins approved of the redesigned bird house; but the squirrel repellant bird feeder worked wonderfully.

Nothing remained small and simple with Daddy. The projects turned into Adirondack chairs with matching tables and footstools. Beautiful swings were made with different designs. Then the furniture projects became even bigger.

Daddy built beautiful entertainment centers and sofa tables with matching side tables. Daddy made the most wonderful cutting boards and even decorative picture frames. Once a family member requested a wooden clothes hamper, so the two of them came up with a plan and built it in a few days time.

But building was only half the job. Daddy wanted to choose the wood. After choosing the type of wood, he would cut and plane the wood himself. So that required a planar. He knew all the tricks to the process of drying and preparing the wood. The wood was not just pine or oak — oh no, Daddy used pecan, mesquite, and cypress. Many times he cut wood from his own land. Occasionally, a family member would bring in exotic mesquite or cypress. In fact, he did not make many outdoor things unless he used cypress.

In our adult life, Christmas gifts always involved something Daddy and Mama made. Mama added her wonderful talents to some of Daddy's projects, as well.

One year, we were all given beautiful cedar chests. What a treasure! But Doug and I own one very special treasure. It is a treasure which no one else owns. My sister and brother received one of Daddy's beautiful swings. I did not have a big yard or porch for a swing, so I decided to talk to Daddy about making a glider. I did have a large outdoor deck so I decided a wooden glider would be great. That project became Daddy's new challenge. Of course, his response was — with the "Oh" at a higher pitch — "Oh Yeah, I can make one."

So make a glider, he did. Daddy had to order a pattern and parts necessary to make the glider swing as it should. Now, I had no clue that there were so many details involved in making a glider.

The hardware necessary to operate a glider was above my ability to understand. The mechanical parts and each piece of wood had to fit together perfectly for the glider to glide. But Daddy was accepting the challenge!

However, a slight mishap caused the process to stall. Daddy always cut and planed the wood for his projects first. Well, he was preparing the oak wood for my glider when somehow the board he was preparing slipped and hit his wrist. Much to my dismay, Daddy's wrist was broken.

Remember, nothing was simple with Daddy. His wrist would not heal, which led to wrist surgery. Then the injury finally healed. The end result was a beautiful handmade — with the cost of injury — oak glider!

Not only that, Mama made beautiful pillows to place on it. Thank goodness, she did not hurt herself making the pillows. Needless to say, this glider will never see the outdoors. It will always be a treasured piece of furniture, but enjoyed only indoors!

I mention all of that just to explain that Daddy enjoyed being busy, and he loved being outdoors. He continued to go outdoors even when he was not in the best of health. We all worried about him hurting himself with the woodwork projects, because healing was slow due to Daddy's illnesses.

Eventually, he was unable to get about on his own. He was too weak to stand alone. His body had become very weak. He could no longer get outdoors. Daddy no longer had energy to ride in his all-terrain vehicle or take a drive in his truck. He no longer had the strength to stand at his work bench and create treasures. Getting outdoors was something Daddy was unable to do, even occasionally.

Many times, when illness and inabilities limit the usual way of life, depression creeps in. Disease attacks and depression threatens happiness. Although Daddy's days were spent indoors now, he filled the time with family and friends.

Daddy knew his earthly body was getting too weak to continue. He knew his body would give out, but he would live for eternity in heaven. His earthly concerns seemed to cause Daddy to worry about the family he would leave behind. He worried about Mama. Daddy knew that my sister, my brother, and I had our spouses and families, but he still was concerned about all of us. Would we be okay?

He would talk to us about being in heaven. He was comforted by God's assurance, but Satan also causes doubt to creep in. That doubt must be conquered through faith in our heavenly Father.

I saw Daddy in turmoil because of an earthly-heavenly struggle. Daddy had faith in God's plans, but he faced new trials. It was as if the Holy Spirit was guiding him to enjoy family and friends with every day he had left on this earth, providing peace and promising life everlasting. Yes, he knew a celebration was in store for him in heaven. He knew Mama Mac, Pop, Aunt Norene, Deborah, and many others were there waiting for him to come home. But the other struggle seemed to be letting go.

Daddy had to let go of his time here on earth. He knew he had to let go of his family and loved ones who would be left behind on earth, even though Daddy knew it would only be a temporary separation. It seemed Daddy was going through a struggle. Perhaps he was walking through darkness. Psalm 23:4 states that,

> Yea, though I walk through the valley of the shadow
> of death, I will fear no evil: for thou art with me;
> thy rod and thy staff they comfort me. (KJV)

The darkness Daddy seemed to be in on this earth caused sadness, depression, and periods of tears. Still, Daddy would again be encouraged because he knew God was with him.

Doug and I made trips to visit him, since Daddy was unable to travel. Sometimes our visits would be for two or three days, but the weaker Daddy got the shorter they got. Usually just for a day.

We would travel for six hours of the day and get little visiting time, but Daddy needed his rest. He rested better if there was no interference in his daily schedule.

So we made more frequent, but shorter visits. Usually a visit would end with me kneeling beside his recliner and telling him, "I love you Daddy." Then Daddy would tell me, "I love you too, Sugar."

As congestive heart failure continued to weaken Daddy, we continued to have day visits. Daddy would sit in his recliner, and we would talk. It became difficult for him to carry on conversations.

Daddy did not have a lot of energy to speak and his words would be slurred. But Daddy never retreated to his bedroom to be by himself. He always sat in his recliner and visited with whomever came to see him. Daddy might nap a little while, but he wanted to make sure he stayed with everyone who visited.

When it was time for Doug and me to leave, Daddy would be filled with sadness. He would say things, but I could not understand everything he said. His words were just mumbles. He would even begin to cry.

He knew his body was very weak. Thoughts of whether he would be here on earth to see us again probably filled his mind. I would kneel down beside his chair as he cried. We talked about trusting in the Lord for all things. Both of us would acknowledge that God is always near to take care of all who believe. But, God's Word lights our path and tells us,

> This is the day which the Lord hath made; we will
> rejoice and be glad in it. (Psalms 118:24 KJV)

We sometimes even sang this verse as we remembered what God promises. Daddy believed this because he believed in God. We drew strength from this promise. This promise provided peace and comfort. The temporary darkness, sadness, and depression would no longer have a place in that moment.

Again I would say, "I love you, Daddy." I always got the response: "I love you too, Sugar."

Miraculously, God pulled Daddy through the dark times. Daddy believed in God the Father. He raised us in a way to believe in the heavenly Father. We were so blessed to have a dedicated earthly daddy and our heavenly Father.

I miss Daddy, but am so happy he is resting with God our Father — healed, happy, and at peace. I believe and have assurance that I will, one day, receive that grace and that promised blessing as well. Praises be to God for providing a place of peaceful, eternal life.

How can anyone pull through the turmoil of this earth without believing in the Lord God almighty? How can anyone not understand He is the maker of heaven and earth?

Oftentimes, people make it through their struggles, but not always successfully. Those who choose to be without God suffer depression, unhappiness, distress and troubles without hope. My heart breaks for people who are so lonely because they choose to be without God.

All I am certain of is that I believe, Daddy believed, and I am in a family that believes. We believe in God's plan for us. That is where I find my comfort and peace in a world of turmoil. The Holy Spirit is with me, surrounding me and in my soul every day.

My family and I were surrounded by God's angels. We were ministered to by God, especially during this particular struggle. Peace, comfort, wisdom, and strength are freely given from God. God's grace was given to us at that particular time and continues to be freely given to all who believe on Him.

People often make comments such as, "I don't know how you do it."

Well, the only way I can explain the strength given is walking in that special place with God. My family and I had a special walk in a place where the Father, Jesus Christ the Son, and the Holy Spirit stay very close — the "thin place."

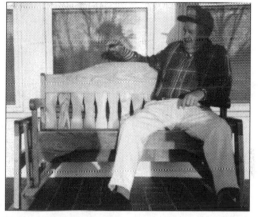

Daddy enjoying sitting on the oak glider he made.
He has a red and white stripped cast on his right wrist
because he broke his wrist while building the glider.

But they that wait upon the Lord shall renew their strength; they shall mount up with wings as eagles; they shall run, and not be weary; and they shall walk, and not faint. (Isaiah 40:31 KJV)

CHAPTER

Happy Birthday!

Summer beaming in the South! What a wonderful, exciting, beautiful, and exhaustingly hot time of the year! The colors of the summer in the South could fill the rainbow. The days are gloriously long. Lazy late afternoons can be spent on the porch, with a ceiling fan working to create a slight breeze for everyone.

Then there are the soothing summer sounds. Hundreds of birds fill the air with glorious song; even the insects hum in the trees. If the Lord blesses the afternoon with a rain shower, crickets sing and frogs bellow out, in harmony.

But oh, the humidity through the summer months in the South can almost become unbearable. The high temperatures of a summer day are bearable, but the heat of the day mixed with humidity is quite an experience.

I might add that it could be an unpleasant experience. The air seems to become so heavy, that even everyone who prefers the outdoors must retreat to the air-conditioned indoors in order to breathe. As wonderful as summer is, one does need to become acclimated to endure this grand season in the South.

Daddy was acclimated to the summertime. In fact, he stayed

out most of the day. Of course, he was a three-meals-a-day person, so breakfast was a must before going out, he would take a break for lunch, the work ended at dinner time.

Many mornings and late afternoons you could find Daddy sitting in a lawn chair, looking out over the pond, catching a nap when needed.

Even as Daddy's health issues began to handicap him, he still enjoyed sitting outside in his lawn chair. But, as I have mentioned, this summer was different. Daddy could not enjoy things as usual because his health hindered his movement.

Those new earthly trials and struggles which Daddy experienced climaxed during the month of June and continued to churn into July. These trials were coming during a time of the year Daddy loved.

The days were warm enough for him to get outdoors now. However, Daddy's health continued to fail. At least, he had been able to sit in his recliner and visit with us during part of the day.

But now some of his days were spent in the bed, getting rest during the day. It seemed so unusual for Daddy to have no interest in getting out of bed.

Eating was something Daddy became less interested in too. We knew he was less active so he needed less food, but he did not even seem interested in eating his favorite foods. The constant sleeping and lack of interest in food was very out of character for Daddy, so it was hard for us to understand his actions or even his needs.

One day, Daddy would get out of bed and sit in his recliner in the den, with some assistance. He enjoyed visiting with family and friends, watching TV, or catching a quick nap. Then, the next two days, he would need to have bed rest. It seemed that rest was needed in order to replace the energy used to visit with family members and friends.

Depression due to the lack of mobility became like a demon torturing Daddy, but the Lord always reminded him that all was well. He, again, would remember the verse,

> This is the day which the Lord hath made; we will rejoice and be glad in it. (Ps. 118:24, KJV)

Daddy continued enjoying all people and things around him. Everyone and everything around him was given by the Lord to provide Daddy strength to continue until the Lord needed him in heaven. As weak as his body was, Daddy was still carrying out the Lord's work for all to see. What an amazing, wonderful thing — the work of the Lord.

Everyone who knew and loved Daddy became concerned. Prayers were always offered up for him and we knew God was with him and us. However, being as self-sufficiently foolish as I sometimes am, I had decided that overnight guests would hinder Daddy's sleep at night. I had decided Doug and I should only have the short, day visits to see Daddy. I had decided, at least pertaining to Doug and myself, after discussing this with Mama, that Daddy might not need a lot of people around for his upcoming birthday. So many things *I had decided*.

In reality, there probably were more things I decided than I have mentioned. Thank the Lord He has humor and provides me with enough humor to laugh at myself.

My eyes have been opened to see my mistakes and be reminded that He is in control. I thought I knew what was best for Daddy and was forgetting God really knew. Praises be to God!

The last of June and going into July, Daddy had become much weaker. Living away from him, I would also visit with Daddy by having short phone conversations.

However, now, his words had steadily become more and more slurred. I could hardly understand his words over the telephone. Mostly, I just listened.

But listening to Daddy talk on the phone, even for a minute, assured me as to how strong or weak he was that day.

Sometimes the words, although few, were understandable; other times the words would be just a mumble. Whether the conversation with Daddy was by phone or by a visit to his house, whether it was hard for him to speak or easy, the last thing I would say was, "I love you Daddy." He would reply, with words I could always understand, no matter how slurred, "I love you too, Sugar."

And now it was the first week in the sweltering month of July. The summer had been unusually hot, even for those of us who have always lived in the South.

This first week in July, when I made my phone calls to Mama and Daddy, Daddy was usually asleep. He would not wake to eat. Mama was trying so hard to cook anything she could think of to tempt Daddy into eating. He was not interested in visiting or talking with people either.

It seemed he had no energy left to do anything so he just stayed in bed and slept. As a result, when I called I was unable to even talk with him over the phone. I was no longer able to detect Daddy's strength through his voice.

Now, most of the phone conversations were with Mama. Daddy had always led a very active life, but now was someone staying in bed, day and night.

Now, physical strength seemed to be leaving Daddy quickly. He did not even have strength for our telephone conversations. And this was not easy.

The days could have been very dismal and depressing for Daddy — and for everyone who loved and cared for him.

However, God provided strength for all of us to continue to be together as a family. God gave all of us the ability to be able to help when needed.

With Daddy's declining health, plans were made for us to travel to visit him, but only for the day. Daddy had a birthday coming up on the fifth of July, and Doug and I were determined to be there.

After conversations with Mama, I knew it would not be the normal birthday event. Daddy always enjoyed a birthday cake. And homemade ice cream was always an absolute necessity.

He was certainly too weak for all of the grandchildren and their families. It would be a birthday with just Mama, Daddy, Doug, and me. My sister and brother and their spouses, who lived nearby, would probably pop in and out during the day.

Looking back now, I was the one who decided crowds were not best for Daddy, now. I thought the day would be spent sitting around the house and waiting to see if Daddy might wake just long enough so I might speak to him. Just being there would still be a good day, and I knew Daddy would want us there for his birthday.

So Doug and I got up early on the fifth of July, quickly prepared to travel for the day, and then drove over to see Daddy for his birthday. We started on our journey unaware of how this day was shaping up.

Remember, it was July and July is in the middle of the wonderful, exciting, beautiful, and exhaustingly hot summertime in the South. It also was another one of those unusually sultry days.

But strange as it may seem, when we arrived Daddy was outside, cruising around on his electric cart. He already had Mama, my sister, and my brother setting up in the shade of the carport for a party.

They already had tables placed and covered with red and

white checked tablecloths. Foldable chairs had been placed around some of the tables for seating. Lawn chairs had been opened and arranged for groups to sit together and visit.

How was all of this happening, especially after a week when Daddy was even too weak to have a conversation with me on the phone? And who all was coming?

Since I was certain that a party had not been planned, Mama had to explain how the day started.

"Happy Birthday to Me, Happy Birthday to Me," were Daddy's words that morning. Daddy did not only remember what day it was, but he was singing "Happy Birthday."

After being bed ridden almost all week, sleeping most of the time, he woke up that morning. Not only did he wake up, but he wanted help getting out of the bed. Daddy was ready to eat breakfast, get his shower and a shave, and get dressed. He reminded her that it was his birthday. How in the world did he remember himself? Wouldn't he naturally lose track of the days in bed?

So Mama did exactly what Daddy had decided to do for the day. She cooked his old-time favorite breakfast of fried eggs, sausage, and toast, and Daddy ate it. Previously, he could not even be tempted by favorite foods.

Then she helped him get dressed. Just the two of them got all of this accomplished that morning. But even getting breakfast and getting dressed was a big deal now. It would usually take the entire morning to get out of bed, eat, and get dressed. But today, my never-the-dull-moment Daddy was having a party. We were having a party. But what party? No one had planned a party and now Daddy expected a party. We were going to have a miraculous birthday party.

Soon, Daddy's grandchildren began to come by, bringing their families. We had the great-grandchildren too — small children and babies everywhere, and Daddy seemed to be having a glorious time.

He had someone find his summer hat and he cruised around on his electric cart, visiting and supervising. An outside party during a week of very hot weather was quite an endeavor! We would all surely melt in the heat, but how would Daddy stand the entire event? But, we were having a glorious, miraculous, mind-boggling birthday party for Daddy.

The chatter of people was heard everywhere, and children were laughing and playing. We were all there with the sensuous smell of hamburgers and hotdogs grilling, and, of course homemade ice cream churning.

I wondered sometimes if Daddy ever knew ice cream could be bought in the store. I do not think he wanted to know that ice cream could be store-bought because he always had Mama make up homemade ice cream, just to keep in the freezer. Someone arrived with a birthday cake and Daddy's birthday party was well on its way.

Everyone started coming in — some lived next door, some lived near, and some lived a good distance away — but everyone was starting to arrive to spend lunch with Daddy at his birthday party.

How did the grandchildren know to come? How was the right amount of food on hand? How did we get a cake? What about the heat outside? How was this happening?

Cruising around on his electric cart, Daddy laughed and seemed to enjoy himself. What a wonderful day it was. Everyone ate, laughed, and had wonderful fellowship together. Not even one person complained about the heat of the day.

Oddly enough, the day had cooled and a breeze blew in the air. We were all amazed at how Daddy was able to talk and laugh, enjoying his birthday with us. The day had turned out to be absolutely perfect in every way and we knew we were all blessed.

Enjoying the wonderful time together, Daddy even remembered to ask about mine and Doug's daughter. Daddy knew her husband was battling cancer and even with his own illness, Daddy was still concerned for them.

And then suddenly, among all of the fellowship, Daddy raised his voice to get everyone's attention. Daddy raised his voice!

As mentioned, Daddy's body was weakening. In addition, his voice weakened and he became unable pronounce words clearly.

He told us, "While I have everyone here, I don't know how much longer I will be here, but I want you to know how much I love you."

In a short speech, Daddy told us he wanted us to know how much he appreciated and loved us.

As hard as this must have been, through tears and expressions of love and joy, Daddy still wanted all of us to know how much he loved us. It seemed the struggles with earthly experiences had subsided.

On this day, his birthday, he used this time to let all of us know he knew he was sick. It was important for him to let us know he was ready to go home.

He knew he would live eternally with God his Father, in his real home. He knew heaven is the ultimate destination for God's people.

This wood worker told us that all he needed was a little cabin in heaven. He needed one where he could wait for his family. He talked to us with laughter and tears. His words were clear, and he spoke in complete sentences. Where had this strength come from? It was as if Daddy knew his God-assigned work was almost complete on this earth. He and God had a plan, and it sounded like a wonderful, glorious plan.

As the party wrapped, grandchildren and great-grandchildren began to leave. Becoming tired, Daddy decided to move inside to his recliner in the den. He needed to take an afternoon nap. My sister, brother, and I, along with our spouses, helped Mama clean up after the birthday party. It had been a beautiful day for a birthday party.

As Doug and I prepared to travel back to our house, Daddy still sat in his recliner, part of the time visiting and part of the time napping. He was tired now, but still sitting up in the recliner — not in the bed. Just before leaving, I knelt beside Daddy's chair to tell him good bye. As usual I said, "I love you Daddy" and, as always, he replied, "I love you too, Sugar."

Daddy may have slept through the week before his birthday, but God had planned a beautiful day for a birthday. We had certainly not planned anything. Remember, I decided Daddy probably only needed his children and their spouses to visit on his birthday. We were amazed how Daddy even had the energy to be up.

Besides Daddy's unusual strength that day, the heat of July had cooled some as well, with a nice breeze in the air. During the birthday party, no one mentioned being uncomfortable — the heat, the bugs, nothing seemed to make anyone uncomfortable. We were all in a place where angels were with us.

God provided all things and His angels were there holding Daddy up that day, giving his body strength. The Holy Spirit was with us, controlling the weather, making us feel comfortable on a southern July day. He brought the power of the Lord to us as always, but we felt it even more that day. The Holy Spirit was pouring over love, joy, peace, patience, gentleness, goodness and faithfulness.

No one had to be invited to Daddy's house for a birthday party. God led us all there. God led people to prepare enough food for the party. God led different individuals to bring in everything that was needed to have a party. God gave words — clear words — for Daddy to talk with us about going home to heaven. His words fell on our ears and we could understand, even though he had been too weak to even speak clearly just days earlier.

Daddy spoke those wonderful words of assurance that we needed to hear in order to be at peace knowing Daddy was at peace. What an amazingly, wonderful, powerful, and loving God we have.

God reminded us that He is in control — God planned a birthday party for Daddy. God provided good rest for Daddy during the days before the birthday party. Only He knew it was just the rest Daddy needed. The birthday party God threw for Daddy provided a time of assurance and love. It was that place where love is all around and nothing can dampen it; a place with God — the "thin place."

Daddy preparing to run from the cattle in
the cattle drive while visiting in Texas.

So don't be anxious about tomorrow. God will take
care of your tomorrow too. Live one day at a time.
(Matthew 6:34 TLB)

CHAPTER

Rest

Then there was rest. Funny thing — God knows how and when we, in our human bodies, need rest. Everyone returned home safely from Daddy's birthday party and Daddy was resting. It is written in the book of Genesis,

> Thus the heavens and the earth were finished, and all the host of them. And on the seventh day God ended his work which he had made; and he rested on the seventh day from all his work which he had made. And God blessed the seventh day, and sanctified it: because that in it he had rested from all his work which God created and made. (Genesis 2:1–3, KJV)

It is interestingly miraculous how God created the heavens, the earth, and all that is in the earth in six days. The fact that the entire creation was completed in six days is more than interestingly miraculous. In fact, it is more than I can even begin to comprehend. Creation is certainly another event that shows the glory and greatness of God.

All can be assured that God is in control, and He can do anything. But on the seventh day He rested. Really? God rested? I wonder sometimes if God really needed a rest.

I think God was just doing something else for us. Perhaps He was simply modeling the importance of rest for all. We probably need to study more in the book of Genesis, in order to understand how God wants us to work and to rest.

God worked to create something wonderfully grand, something to share. He worked and created for six days. Maybe He was demonstrating how work should be done, but then God rested. It is written in Mark 2: 27–28,

> And he (Jesus Christ) said unto them, "The sabbath was made for man, and not man for the sabbath: Therefore the Son of man is Lord also of the Sabbath." (KJV)

God also instructed Moses, one of His great prophets, to explain to His people the importance of rest. In Exodus, it is written,

> Six days thou shalt do thy work, and on the seventh day thou shalt rest: that thine ox and thine ass may rest, and the son of thy handmaid, and the stranger, may be refreshed. (Exodus 23:12 KJV)

So God instructed that even the animals should be given time to rest. Many Scriptures explain the importance of rest and meditation for all of creation. I believe God modeled this for all to understand, just as He continues to do in the present.

So with God in control of every ounce of Daddy's body, he rested. For the next two days, Daddy rested. But praise God he had the strength to enjoy his birthday party.

Daddy did not have strength like a healthy person — getting up and walking around — but God provided all the strength Daddy needed to get dressed. God provided Daddy with energy to visit and laugh and talk. Daddy even had the desire to eat.

Daddy had the appetite to eat his breakfast, in order to energize his body. He had an appetite to eat a piece of his birthday cake, a bowl of homemade ice cream, and a hamburger. Daddy had energy and an appetite that none of us had seen for a long time. God provided Daddy with all he needed to have a good time.

So now, Daddy rested. His rest lasted days with little to eat through Sunday and Monday. Anxiety takes hold when loved ones become uninterested in eating or waking. We all worry because there is nothing but sleep; there is no response, just sleep. God knew Daddy needed little food and much rest and so God provided it all.

But Monday was another low and inactive day for Daddy. I could understand that Daddy needed his rest on Sunday. We all knew that just a visit with someone would drain Daddy's energy.

I should have remembered that much rest was needed. I should have remembered that God always has us in the palm of His hand and would continue to keep us safe there. I guess I did not understand that Daddy would probably need more rest this time. After all, he attended his birthday party, not just a mere one-day visit.

The home health care nurses and aides were always so attentive to Daddy. They were always helping Mama to provide the perfect care he needed. But Daddy continued to stay in bed and sleep.

As mentioned before, the habit of staying in bed was not a normal habit for Daddy. So on Monday I received a phone call to inform me of Daddy's condition. It was not a phone call in which I could speak to him and hear the strength in his voice. Just like before his birthday party, he was not waking, eating, or talking.

So Monday was one of those phone tag days. You know, one of those long days filled with calls and contacts. Those days when loved ones are sick, but you live away from home, so you have to listen to the opinions of others over the phone. You can't be there to see loved ones or hear them yourself.

I was not there to see Daddy for myself that Monday so I had to make many calls during the day to check on him. During the calls, I would get information about how Daddy was doing. I was told he was okay at the moment and someone would call me when I was needed.

Between calls I would wonder what was going on there. The only thing I knew to do was to get on my knees and pray. So that's what I did. I knew to trust in the Lord and I knew that He was with all of us, but human nature set in that day and my concern was heavy.

My spiritual mind was not focused at that time. God provided rest for Daddy, but my earthly thoughts caused me to decide he should be awake by now. As I think about it now, I am reminded to always pray that my spiritual eyes, mind, and heart will always be guided by the Lord God. At that time, I failed to understand that God knew Daddy needed extra rest.

So Doug and I had just driven over on Saturday for Daddy's birthday and now it was only Monday, but I felt the need to be there again.

Working in education, Doug and I were able to be flexible with plans during the summer months, so Tuesday we decided to travel over again to see Daddy. But this time, we planned to stay a few days. I do not know why we decided to stay this time, but sometimes God moves in ways we don't understand. Proverbs 20:24 states,

Since the Lord is directing our step, why try to understand everything that happens along the way? (TLB)

What a wonderful and unexplainable peace and comfort this word from God does bring to my very soul. So we packed to stay a few days and left Tuesday morning to travel to see Mama and Daddy.

Daddy vacationing and visiting family in Texas.

Trust in the Lord with all thine heart; and lean not unto thine own understanding. In all thy ways acknowledge him, and he shall direct thy paths. (Proverbs 3:5–6, KJV)

CHAPTER

Surprise!

Tuesday, when Doug and I arrived safely, again, to Mama and Daddy's house, no one greeted us when we came through the door. Everyone knew we were traveling back over.

The kitchen door was open, so we walked in. The kitchen was empty so we walked out of the kitchen, through the wash room, and into the hallway leading to the bedrooms.

As we entered the hallway, Doug and I heard conversations coming from Mama and Daddy's bedroom. It was Mama with my brother, sister, and their spouses. But much to my amazement, Daddy was sitting up talking with them!

Daddy was awake, sitting up, and having conversation with everyone! Sure, his speech was slurred and he was too weak to get out of bed or even hold himself up, but he was awake, sitting up, and talking!

After his birthday, Daddy slept for two days and three nights. Doug and I arrived at Mama and Daddy's house about lunchtime and Daddy was awake. No one had called to let me know Daddy was awake, but I understood why —everyone was occupied visiting with Daddy. Laughter was in the room again. What a wonderful surprise!

As Doug and I walked through the bedroom door, Daddy's voice greeted us. Of course, his speech was slurred and Daddy had some confusion after waking, but he definitely greeted Doug and me as we walked into his bedroom. It was a somewhat different greeting because he shouted, "Hey!" His voice was very strong.

I could tell Daddy was a little confused because for a moment it seemed that he must have thought I was Mama. But many people tell me that I look a lot like my mother.

Daddy watched as my husband, Doug, walked over to his bed. Mama attempted to remind Daddy that it was Doug, but before she completed her introduction, Daddy looked directly at Doug and said, "Hey, Doug."

In fact, the salutation was even more pronounced than his greeting to me. Since he knew who Doug was, being his son-in-law, it occurred to me that he also knew exactly who I was.

We learned from the others that he had just woken up. My sister said the names of everyone in the room for Daddy to make sure he knew who was there. Although he seemed a little confused and was slurring his words, Daddy was sitting up on the side of his bed and talking.

He probably thought we were the ones confused, making such to do over him waking up. Amazed, I had to process again the fact that he had not woken or eaten in three nights and two days, and now he was sitting on the side of his bed.

My sister sat on one side of Daddy and Mama sat on the other side. It was necessary for them to steady him as he was still weak. This allowed him the stability to sit on the side of the bed, resting his feet on the floor.

It was important to Daddy to be able to sit on the edge of the bed, with his feet touching the floor, even though he could not get out of the bed. But it was so wonderful to see Daddy talking and laughing again. What had changed?

The previous two days, no one had been able to awaken Daddy. He must have been in a deep, God-given rest — the rest he needed to recover. But now he was awake. God gave Daddy the energy to attend his birthday party on Saturday, and then provided him with the rest he needed.

Daddy sat on the side of his bed and talked with all of us for a good while. However, it seemed at times that Daddy still had some confusion on this Tuesday morning, although, I still wonder now if we may have been the confused.

I think about this because one very different and interesting incident happened as we visited with Daddy. During our conversations, Daddy began to look as if seeing something or someone behind our little circle of people.

Daddy started to mumble a few words. I noticed he was starting to show aggravation on his face and my sister noticed too. Then everyone in the room noticed Daddy's odd, insistent questions.

As we all silenced and tried to help, he pointed behind me and clearly asked, "Who is that woman?" It was evident he was not talking about me, or anyone standing around me. I tried to tell him there was not a woman there. Daddy continued to peer around us. I explained to him that he must be seeing the furniture behind me. But Daddy insisted he wanted to know who that woman was. Everyone tried to convince him that no one was there except us, but that did not seem to satisfy him.

Since he was slurring his speech it was difficult to understand everything Daddy was trying to tell us about the woman standing behind us. Eventually, because of our ignorance and his lack of strength, Daddy stopped asking about the woman.

Did he see a woman? Why did he mention a "woman" and not

a man? As sick a Daddy was, I felt some concern for this strange incident, but oddly enough, now I find some comfort in it. It comforts me to think that Daddy received the ability to see pleasant things with his spiritual eyes. Perhaps I was not able to see with my spiritual eyes what Daddy could see.

After resting in the Lord for two days, Daddy not only woke up ready to visit with us, but he also was ready to eat breakfast. He woke with an appetite. Of course, He had been asleep for days and now he was hungry.

Mama prepared him a grand breakfast, although it was noon by this time. But Daddy was a person who had to start the day off with a breakfast meal, no matter what time he started his day. If he ever had to fast because of doctor's orders before a medical test, Daddy would immediately follow the test appointment with breakfast regardless of the time of day. So with our help, he did enjoy eating his fried eggs. The Lord, once again, provided Daddy with blessed rest.

Of course, Daddy could only sit up for short periods of time, and then he would rest back on his pillows. Daddy was not able to get up from his bed and move to his favorite recliner in the den, but he could sit up on the side of his bed. And his body still had pain and weakness.

Daddy still had to have assistance sitting up, but he enjoyed sitting on the side of his bed, with us around, and having his feet firmly planted on the floor. Oh, how we enjoyed visiting with him. Daddy talked and laughed with us, and although we might not understand everything he said, he knew exactly what he was talking about.

When he became tired of sitting on the side of the bed, Daddy would tell us to stack up his pillows so he could recline in the bed. He would rather sit up in his bed, reclining on pillows, rather than lie down in the bed. We would always stay with him until he dosed off, and then we would let him rest.

God always provided rest for Daddy — provided him rest because He knew Daddy enjoyed being with his family so much. Rest brought the energy needed to have this precious time. Laughter, love, family, and God were with us in this "thin place."

Daddy having coffee while enjoying friends and
family after a day of fishing in Alaska.

And this is what God says we must do: Believe
on the name of his Son Jesus Christ, and love one
another. Those who do what God says — they are
living with God and he with them. We know this
is true because the Holy Spirit he has given us tells
us so. (1 John 3:23—24 TLB)

Enjoying Time Together

The next morning, Wednesday morning, Daddy slept a little late, but he woke again that day. So now we all had another day in which we could all visit with Daddy.

Although Daddy was awake on Tuesday when we arrived and Doug and I decided to stay a few days, we continued to have concerns of tiring Daddy with a long visit. I already knew through phone conversations with Mama that Daddy was not resting well most nights.

Mama told me Tuesday night was one of those nights. Daddy had been awake a good bit of the night, although I never heard him, though we were staying in the house. As a result, Daddy slept late into the morning, and Mama was very tired.

Even though Daddy had been unresponsive on Sunday and Monday, he awoke some on Tuesday and even again on Wednesday. Wow!

And when he did wake, he requested breakfast again. How wonderful it was to hear him put in a request for food. Daddy ate some of his beloved fried egg for breakfast, and then spent the entire morning awake. Staying awake long periods of time had become quite difficult for him to do now.

His "busy" morning was partly due to his wonderful home health care aide. She came in to give him the home health care "spa treatment." She had been coming in for some time now, and much to our amazement, Daddy had learned to enjoy that special treatment. Isn't it always nice to see God at work, adjusting our preferences as needed?

Daddy enjoyed getting cleaned up and shaved. He was the type of person who always wanted a shave and a shower. He had become very dependent on Mama for all things, but much to our surprise, Daddy's home health care aide became a good friend to him.

It is not often easy to accept help from nurses coming into the home. I cannot even count the number of times Daddy made the comment that he did not need a home health care aide. Daddy had always been very private about attending to his own hygiene habits. But he had developed a close friendship with this amazing lady who was coming into his home to help Mama take care of him. There are not enough words to describe the wonderful help and positive support the home health care professionals provide. I fully believe these positions are callings from God.

Home health care nurses and staff accept God's call to do special work for sick people and their families. The Lord provides all that is needed for them to do this work.

This visit does not seem to involve much activity, but for Daddy it was a workout. Daddy accomplished more that Wednesday morning than he had in quite a few days.

Afterwards, Daddy needed a massage. He had a great deal of pain and stiffness in the neck and shoulders. This pain was probably partly due to the fact that he had no strength to get up and walk around. He really did not even have enough strength to hold up his shoulders and head, so we would have to reposition him on the pillows which propped him up in his bed.

You see, when Daddy sat up his head would hang over, causing stiffness. Being in the bed too long seemed to cause him to also hurt in his back and hips. Though I have no medical or therapy degree, I still wanted to try something which might relieve Daddy of some of his discomfort.

So this time when Doug and I visited, I brought over a mineral spray and rub to try to bring relief to Daddy's tired muscles. Who knows if all that stuff really works, but sometimes it's necessary to try just about anything when loved ones are in pain.

Tuesday night was our first experience with the mineral spray massage. And he liked it! So after his home health care spa treatment, he was now ready for me to give him his neck and shoulder rub. His skin was very fragile and I had to be careful not to burn or tear his skin. But we were all willing to do anything to make Daddy comfortable. It made me feel good too when Daddy told me he felt better after I rubbed down his neck and shoulders.

We were all so thankful that Daddy had a better day on Wednesday. He had to sleep most of the afternoon to get needed rest, but he had stayed awake all morning. He was able to eat and visit with his friend from home health care. The health care aide seemed to be so pleased that Daddy was feeling better.

After resting through the afternoon, Daddy did wake up to eat a little more. What a blessing it was for us to see him eat again, even just a little. Then about bedtime, he was ready for another neck and shoulder rub. It must be so uncomfortable, always staying in the bed, only sitting up occasionally. However, we all were able to visit with each other again, and even though Daddy was limited to his bed, he did so much to lift our spirits and make all of us feel better. Daddy was still doing work for God on this earth. We were blessed with another good day.

Although Tuesday night, Daddy did not wake Doug and me

with his sleeplessness, Wednesday night was very different. Daddy napped on and off through the afternoon on Wednesday, however, as he napped he was very restless and appeared to be in pain. Then throughout Wednesday night, I could hear Daddy talking to Mama about how he was hurting and needed to move.

I got up and walked into their bedroom to offer to help. The light was on and Mama was trying to roll Daddy over to try to ease his pain. Daddy was too weak to help her. Mama, being of very small frame herself, was struggling to move him. However, together, she and I were able to shift Daddy around a little easier. This went on most of Wednesday night.

Sometimes Mama and I were unable to move Daddy, so Doug would help us reposition Daddy. Being there 24 hours of the day, I began to understand what a struggle they were having at night trying to rest. What love it takes for spouses and family to keep loved ones at home when their loved ones are ill and weak. However, Mama did whatever was needed, with family helping her occasionally, and whatever was needed, the Lord gave everyone strength.

It was good to be with Mama and Daddy on Tuesday afternoon after he woke from those days of sleeping. Then on Wednesday, it was good to be with everyone again, enjoying Daddy's company. Just imagine the relief Doug and I felt that Tuesday morning when we arrived to see Daddy sitting up, talking, and even later, requesting food. The strength we have, especially in dark and emotionally stressful times, is strength which can only come from the Lord.

And so, again, I wonder to myself: Who was really confused on Tuesday when Daddy said things we did not understand or comprehend? Maybe we were the ones in confusion. Perhaps it would have been wonderful to see the woman Daddy was seeing.

Was he still resting comforted — a state given by the Lord? He and all of us were most certainly still being held in the palm of God's hand. I wonder, now, if Daddy was in that "thin place," without us. Perhaps, at that time, we could not see with our eyes and hearts in the same way Daddy could see. Praises to God in all places!

Daddy helping our daughter learn to ride a bike

Fear not, for I am with you. Do not be dismayed. I am your God. I will strengthen you; I will help you; I will uphold you with my victorious right hand. (Isaiah 41:10 TLB)

8

CHAPTER

Stay Another Day?

We all slept a little later on Thursday morning. After all, Wednesday night was an active night for all of us. But we did *all* wake that morning — Daddy too. Praises be to God! I still thought we did not need to have long visits because we would tire Daddy. However, for some reason, that did not seem important anymore.

Doug and I planned to attend a family reunion, one of those big, southern family get-togethers, with his family on Saturday. Thank goodness they planned it on the Saturday following Daddy's birthday and not on the previous Saturday.

Just another way God was at work.

Since this reunion was in a small town near Mama and Daddy, we decided to stay for another day. It would be a shorter distance to travel over to visit Doug's family than it would be from our own house. So we started a new day together; another blessed and wonderful day.

Although we all were a little tired and Daddy was, of course, always in some pain, we were able to enjoy the day. Our days may not have been perfect or wonderful in the eyes of others, but we were enjoying another day together.

I was delighted to be able to help Daddy with his breakfast. Mama cooked him his favorite (fried eggs) and he enjoyed breakfast, again. It was so nice to watch Daddy enjoy eating. Eating breakfast was such a simple thing, yet this simple thing was such a grand event for us. This simple activity provided just a glimmer of improvement to all of us.

Then Daddy had his periods of usual napping to get the rest he needed to sustain him. But afterwards, he and I did get a chance to sit on the side of his bed. I had to hold him up by sitting next to him, using my body for him to lean against. His skin had become so tender that holding or grabbing onto him would cause his skin to tear or bruise.

What a wonderful and precious time we had together! Daddy sat beside me and prayed long prayers. I could not understand all of his words, but that did not matter. Daddy knew he was talking to his Lord and Savior, I knew who he was talking to, and most importantly, our Lord God knew exactly what Daddy was saying — every word.

Daddy was sharing with me his loving relationship with God the Father, and the Holy Spirit was with us at that very moment. God tells us in His Word of His desire to have a relationship with His people. In the Book of Acts it is written,

> That they should seek the Lord, if haply they might
> feel after him, and find him, though he be not far
> from every one of us. (Acts 17:27 KJV)

God is not far away and is ready to have a loving relationship with us. We should seek Him. He is near! I believe that within this relationship we can have conversations with God. It is written,

> Don't worry about anything; instead, pray about
> everything; tell God your needs and don't forget
> to thank him for his answers. If you do this you
> will experience God's peace, which is far more
> wonderful than the human mind can understand.
> His peace will keep your thoughts and your hearts
> quiet and at rest as you trust in Christ Jesus.
> (Philippians 4:6—7 TLB)

Daddy had that relationship with God and God was with him always! He carried on a continuous conversation with God through prayer. Even when words sounded like mumbles, God understood. Praises be to God the Father!

You know, even though Daddy wanted to pray, he also wanted to sing. However, Daddy decided he would prefer for me to sing something for him. One good song, just to get us through tough days became, "This is the Day That the Lord Hath Made,"[1] which is just one more wonderful scripture put to song. Again, it is that scripture that always provided encouragement.

> This is the day that the Lord hath made; we will
> rejoice and be glad in it. (Psalms 118:24 KJV)

Another old favorite song we shared together was "I'll Fly Away."[2] What a wonderful reminder that we will be with the Lord in eternity. God's Word also informs all people to sing songs and give praise. So that is exactly what Daddy and I spent time together doing. What wonderful times the Lord blessed us with. Seemingly simple times, but actually huge, grand times!

After prayers and songs, Daddy was ready to lie back on his pillows to rest. Daddy seemed to enjoy himself, and I truly did.

Mama, Doug, and I sat in the room as Daddy nodded off to sleep, and we began to discuss where we might place an order for lunch. There was no need in anyone cooking today. My goodness, all of us had worked enough through the night trying to move Daddy around in his bed to relieve his pain. Daddy certainly had his workout with us tugging and pulling on him. So Doug and I finally convinced Mama to do take-out for lunch.

I sat on the bed by Daddy as he rested. Actually, I just thought Daddy had dosed off, because while we talked about different restaurants and foods, Daddy answered. He spoke up and said, "I know what I would like."

With amazement, we all got silent and listened. We were probably all a funny sight as we listened with surprised expressions and dropped jaws.

Daddy said, "I would like fried oysters." What? Fried oysters? This was amazing!

Daddy always enjoyed a good plate of fried oysters — as long as he had saltine crackers and plenty of ketchup to eat with them. But he had not wanted any of his favorite foods or much food at all, in weeks. No one even thought of asking Daddy his opinion about lunch.

Honestly, the thought of eating fried oysters was very unappetizing to me, and I even felt I needed to ask Mama if Daddy should eat them. Her response was, "If that's what he wants to eat!" It was so exciting for us to hear Daddy ask for something to eat. The home health care nurse told us he would naturally stop enjoying his favorite foods; and, as mentioned, getting Daddy to eat had become quite a chore.

So Doug and I left on a journey to find fried oysters for Daddy and something else for the rest of us. As we left, Daddy settled in for his very needed nap.

Upon returning from our lunch journey, Daddy was still napping. Allowing him to rest, we all decided to eat our lunch. After we had our lunch, we were able to wake Daddy so he could have his oysters. I sat on the bed next to him as he ate.

He enjoyed his fried oysters and ketchup, along with a few saltine crackers. Daddy would put ketchup on just about anything, and enjoy whatever he was eating. Daddy ate almost the entire order of oysters. We were astonished!

He had to eat sitting in his bed, but eat he did!

Most of all, we enjoyed watching him eat again. Of course, after eating breakfast and lunch, praying, laughing, crying, and visiting, Daddy had to rest. His sleep carried him through a good, restful afternoon.

While Daddy slept, I needed to get a chocolate pie cooked. Doug and I had the family reunion on Saturday and these southern family gatherings required lots of food and plenty of desserts.

As mentioned, the drive would not be far from Mama and Daddy's house, so we decided to stay with Mama and Daddy until it was time to head to the reunion. Afterwards, we could travel back to our house from there.

This visit had been different — it did not seem to exhaust Daddy to have company like before; in fact, he seemed to be slightly more active.

I was able to make Daddy a chocolate pie, as well. Daddy absolutely loved chocolate pie. I am not quite sure if he enjoyed chocolate pie as much as fried oysters, however, if I was going to cook a chocolate pie to take to the reunion; Daddy was going to get one too.

I mention this because I really do not know any reason why I thought I needed to do the pies on Thursday rather than Friday. To have fresh pies, I normally bake the day before I need them. It just worked best, in this situation, to make the pies two days before I needed them.

So we planned to stay another night. Daddy was asleep during the afternoon, so while he slept, I cooked pies. God had planned things just right. What a morning that warmed our hearts! What a walk in the "thin place" with God!

CHAPTER

Making a Move

So on Thursday afternoon, as Daddy rested, I baked chocolate pies. While I worked in the kitchen, my brother and sister came to visit with their spouses. Some of the grandsons also came by. Well, good strong grandsons were good company to have because we needed strong muscles to help us move furniture.

There was a decision made on Wednesday which required helpers on Thursday afternoon.

When the home health care nurse came by on Wednesday, Mama discussed with her the pain and discomfort Daddy was having. The nurse mentioned that a hospital bed could be brought in for Daddy. She seemed to think he might have better rest at night and be able to sit up better when he was awake. In addition, the hospital bed may make night time rest easier for Mama, as well. So after Daddy agreed to the bed, we all started making plans for a furniture moving day.

God had a plan. We thought it was ours; but as always, it was God's good plan. You see, our plan included the wrong day. The nurse mentioned the bed to us on Wednesday. So a call was made to the home health equipment store on Wednesday. The store manager thought the delivery could be made on that very same day.

At first, we were excited that the delivery could be made quickly, but my brother and I realized we did not have enough help since heavy bedroom furniture would need moving. So a delivery date was set for Thursday. All of the siblings and spouses along with some of the grandchildren could help on Thursday. Thursday seemed to be the best day to plan the delivery. It was certain to work because it was God's plan.

I should also mention that this was not the first time Daddy's nurse mentioned a hospital bed. No, originally he did not want a hospital bed. He strongly expressed that he would sleep in his own bed!

So the suggestion of bringing in a hospital bed had to be discussed with Daddy again. After discussing the new bed with Daddy, he decided he would try the bed. Daddy was determined not to have a hospital bed delivered to the house for him to sleep, because, again, he demanded he could sleep in his own bed, but now he had changed his mind.

Daddy thought it might be easier for him to sit up or even get himself up out of bed. We were blessed that, even though weak in body, Daddy was still strong in mind. Since he had been strongly against the idea, it surprised us that he agreed to try the hospital bed.

So on Thursday, the day God planned, we had a moving day. It was a day when all plans seemed to work out smoothly and plenty of people were able to come and help. It was a day where God worked every detail out.

Early in the afternoon on Thursday, my brother and sister came to the house ready to help and Daddy was napping in his bed. After all, he had been up practically all morning. In addition, Thursday was the day he requested the order of fried oysters and had eaten almost the entire order. But we were all going to move the bedroom furniture which needed to be moved to make way for the hospital bed.

Although Daddy was still resting, we started working in the room, hoping Daddy would continue to rest while we worked. But Daddy woke to watch from his bed as we moved furniture around. He belted out a few suggestions of his own.

Daddy wanted to be positioned so he could see the television. A view out the window was also a must-have for him. Throwing in quite a few jokes and laughs, Daddy was a big help to us, in his own way.

There was also some cleaning necessary. We all wanted to make sure that Daddy was perfectly satisfied with his new bed. We were able to get everything accomplished, and then at the right time, the bed was delivered late Thursday afternoon.

After the delivery of the bed, Mama made it up and had it ready for Daddy. As we cleaned and moved furniture, she went out to the store to purchase a new mattress cover to help make the hospital bed a little more comfortable.

The next move was to get Daddy from his bed and into the hospital bed. One of the grandsons was strong enough to move him around without having to grab onto Daddy's arms. We were still very careful not to have much contact with Daddy's fragile skin in order to avoid severely bruising him.

It was quite a struggle to get Daddy from his bed to the hospital bed, even though the two beds were not far apart. Daddy was so weak he could not help move himself, at all. We knew Daddy could not help us lift him back onto his pillows in the bed, but we did not imagine him so weak.

When we did get Daddy moved, he could look outside and see the television, just as he requested. He could even do both at the same time if he wanted! Nevertheless, God's plan was working. God provided extra strength to move Daddy to the hospital bed. It seems that all things do work smoothly together, if it is God's plan.

Having a hospital bed did allow us to position Daddy's head and feet so that he could sit up better. Having the ability to move the head and foot of the bed allowed Daddy some relief by getting off of pressure points which were creating the pain in his back, legs, and hips.

He was able to be awake and have conversation with us. Then Daddy would doze for a while. But he did seem to be very tired from this busy day. Daddy could only stay awake for very short periods of time. It was as if we were going back into an extended period of sleeping with no activity. We always worried when he seemed to want to sleep all the time. But we hoped he would rest better and with less pain now.

As some family members left later in the evening, Mama became very concerned, because Daddy had gone back into such an unresponsive sleep. She was able to talk by phone with the home health care nurse and let her know Daddy was sleeping a lot, again. She also wanted to let the nurse know about the hospital bed, as well.

Were we giving him enough medication to comfort him? Or were we giving him too much medication? This is a constant struggle when trying to care for sick loved ones. Naturally, Mama was always so concerned about how she should medicate Daddy.

I was so glad we were blessed with a wonderful nurse who was able to calm Mama's concerns. Many times, we forget that God always knows when we need rest, and certainly God was with Daddy.

After a while, Mama was able to get some response from Daddy. Was he hungry? We were all concerned that he might need something to eat. Mama asked him if he wanted a taste of his chocolate pie I had cooked for him. He nodded his head. Yes! He finally gave her a response.

So I cut a piece of pie and Mama put a small spoon of it to Daddy's mouth. He tasted it and seemed to enjoy his bite of pie. But as he swallowed, he became choked. He wanted it, but couldn't seem to swallow. It was frightening when he began to choke, but Mama was finally able to ease Daddy and get his throat cleared. We knew he had eaten well that day and, although we were greatly concerned, we knew from past experience that now he was tired and would eat when he needed.

Later, in the evening on Thursday, we had a surprise visitor. Daddy's wonderful home health care nurse came by to check-in. It was seven o'clock in the evening. I wondered if she ever rested at all.

Daddy was lying in the hospital bed for the first night and he was sleeping. He still had not woken up since trying to taste the chocolate pie. The nurse checked on the hospital bed and instructed us on how to adjust the head and the foot of the bed.

Her instructions were very helpful. She showed us how to adjust the head and the foot of the bed so that Daddy would not slip down too far into the bed. Daddy's nurse was such an attentive nurse. She touched Daddy's toes and he responded by only twitching his legs. She informed us that the movement of Daddy's legs indicated he was not in a peaceful rest, so she gave him the full dosage of his medication.

We had decided earlier not to give a full dose because of the fear of overdosing. His nurse knew he needed all of his medication in order to rest without pain. She knew the unresponsive sleep was not because of the medication. It was such a relief that the nurse was there to administer the medication Daddy needed and give us more information.

This home health care nurse did not just happen to come by and check on Daddy. She came because Daddy needed her, we needed her, and our dear God in heaven sent her. What a comfort she was — a comfort sent from God.

God made all the plans for that day. He changed our plans and added His plans. We were all walking among sweet, comforting angels. We were all given comfort once again in the "thin place."

My Daddy, Cecil G. McIntyre.

For I (Paul) am convinced that nothing can ever separate us from his love. Death can't, and life can't. The angels won't, and all the powers of hell itself cannot keep God's love away. Our fears for today, our worries about tomorrow, or where we are — high above the sky, or in the deepest ocean — nothing will ever be able to separate us from the love of God demonstrated by our Lord Jesus Christ when he died for us. (Romans 8:38–39 TLB)

CHAPTER

Peace

Paul wrote to us in 2 Thessalonians 3:16:

> May the Lord of peace himself give you his peace
> no matter what happens. The Lord be with you
> all. (TLB)

To read, think, and know that the Lord of peace gives us His peace is truly amazing and comforting. He is the Lord of peace — it is His peace which will be given if only we believe and ask. Well, Daddy did ask.

He asked that day we prayed together. Daddy's words were mumbles, but I could hear some of them very plainly. Daddy was so very tired. He knew God was with him, and he knew God watched over all of his family.

Daddy had some depression earlier in his sickness. I believe he went through such an inner struggle between his earthly desires and his heavenly desires. So many people face death without fear it seems, but it is still hard to even wrap my mind around how emotional it would be to know that your own weak, human body could not stay on earth much longer.

But this struggle was not because Daddy was afraid of death. He was not concerned for himself, but for the family he would leave behind. Thank the Lord of Peace, I believe He reminded Daddy we live in the palm of God's hand when we receive His peace, grace, and acknowledge He is God.

It is written by Jesus' apostles many times in God's Word that Jesus referred to the dead as "asleep." Jesus referred to the people who others thought were dead, and maybe even had been dead for days, as merely "asleep." Jesus raised Lazarus, from what people called as the dead, but in John 11:11, Jesus said,

> These things said he: and after that he saith unto
> them, "Our friend Lazarus sleepeth; but I go, that
> I may awake him out of sleep." (KJV)

In another instance, Jairus, one of the rulers of the synagogue in the time of Jesus, came asking Jesus to heal his daughter. Before reaching the house where Jairus's daughter lay, Jesus received word that Jairus's daughter had died. When entering the house where the girl lay, Jesus said,

> And when he was come in, he saith unto them,
> "Why make ye this ado, and weep? the damsel is
> not dead, but sleepeth." (Mark 5:39 KJV)

Jesus came to save all who believe, and Jesus came to bring God's wonderful peace. And now, on this Friday morning, Daddy seemed to be completely, mind and body, in that peace.

On Friday morning, neither Mama nor I could wake Daddy. He was still sleeping as solidly and peacefully as when his home health care nurse left him the night before. Daddy's nurse did not leave him until she knew he was in this comforted state of rest — rest without pain.

You see, even though Daddy's eyes were not open, his feet and legs would wiggle or jerk slightly, especially when touched. We learned that this was a sign that he might not be resting well. A new day had started and we thought he might need to eat something; however, we let him rest.

This Friday morning was similar to the other mornings that week. We all had helped move the hospital bed the night before so some family members were stopping by to visit that morning. Everyone was anxious to see if Daddy rested well during his first night in the hospital bed.

My brother and his wife came by. Then my sister came by with her husband. We were all able to get breakfast and enjoy the company of each other. Daddy slept all night Thursday night after his home health care nurse visited, and he continued to rest into the morning. Daddy had spent much of Wednesday and Thursday awake so his body needed rest.

As mentioned before, during the past few months, if Daddy had busy days, days where he would wake and sit up for some time, then the next day or two he needed to spend most of the day sleeping. We all learned that through experience and had come to accept that he would sleep all day.

Daddy's wonderful home health care aide came in to help him with his morning routine, but she decided to do other things so Daddy could rest, continuing to monitor Daddy as she stayed busy. She could always find some way to help. She was a resourceful and caring lady.

I think she just had so much experience working with patients that she just knew what needed to be done. I also believe that it is not only due to experience, but to desire to help others and compassion for patients which makes all home health care professionals so efficient. Anyway, it was a comfort to have her there. Although not a nurse, she was very experienced with handling people suffering from illness.

On this particular morning, we knew breakfast would be served later in the day to him. So we were all together. All of us were there together in Daddy's house, with each other. Doug and I had just eaten breakfast with Mama. We usually prepared fried eggs and toast for Daddy, and we served him breakfast at whatever time of the morning he wanted to eat.

I visited with the other family members in the kitchen while I cleaned our breakfast dishes and put them away.

Mama and my sister walked back to the bedroom where Daddy was. They wanted to check with the home health care aide to see if she noticed if Daddy was awake. The aide was still working around the room, watching over Daddy.

A short time later, a shocking scream caused me to run from the kitchen into the bedroom.

With all of us in the house together on that Friday morning, with Mama, my sister, and the aide in Daddy's bedroom, Daddy took his last breath on this earth. Daddy had come to that place where his mind and soul were both at peace.

Daddy's body had slipped into the sleep that Jesus Christ our Lord had referred to while He was on earth. Daddy's breaths came slower and slower, until finally, Daddy was asleep, resting in God the Father.

It seemed there was no more inner struggle over leaving family, but only his desire to be in heaven. Daddy had reached the peace of the Lord of Peace! There was no more pain and discomfort — only peace.

As I ponder now, I believe Daddy found the total and absolute assurance which God the Father gives. To me it felt as if angels cradled him in peace as he reached for the hand of the Lord, there in that room.

I could feel the angels there. I could feel them there, along with the strength of the Holy Spirit. Daddy showed no sign of pain or discomfort, no sign of resistance, only rest. The total peace we all desire — simple, gracious, but yet glorious. Surely it is a peace that comes when God assures us our work on earth is done. All is good!

We must have been among the angels. No one said anything, but somehow we knew to join together around Daddy's bed. No one said a word for several minutes, only tears for missing our beloved Daddy.

The brush of the angels moved all around, around all of us standing at Daddy's bed as we gave him to be with God. No one asked for anyone to move, no one motioned for anyone to move, but we all ended up circled around Daddy's bed, holding on to each other.

The only thing I felt I could do was pray. I needed to pray among the tears of sorrow for our loss. But first I felt the need to praise God because He was with my Daddy.

Daddy had overcome his walk through the valley of the shadow of death. Praise God, Daddy had overcome the struggle! He found the place where he could hear God, and have full assurance that God was in control. All would be well. Praise God, Daddy was in no more pain. No worry. No struggle.

Daddy had fulfilled his work on God's earth, all of the work God assigned him. Now he was going home, just as Daddy had talked about at his birthday party. Daddy was going home.

We were all in the "thin place" in that instant. We were in the place where heaven came down to earth, and our Lord reached out to welcome Daddy. I believe the Lord came closer to Daddy at that point than ever before.

Daddy was always close to God, but perhaps at that particular time, Daddy saw something he recognized. Maybe Daddy was so close to God he saw something he did not want to be without anymore. He must have seen his home with God.

We all were in that place where there was only God's time; in that place where nothing else mattered and all was rested in the Lord. Time did not matter. Surely, we were in a "thin place" with God and where His Holy Spirit surrounded us!

Oddly enough, although it was a time of great loss for those of us left on earth without Daddy, I felt it to be a time of calmness. It must be a time only experienced by those who believe in the Lord Jesus Christ and God the Father. But in that time, in that "thin place," Daddy was able to receive his reward for being a good and faithful servant. Even Jesus Christ himself speaks of the angels.

In John 1:51, Jesus Christ was gathering His disciples. As He greeted Nathanael, He spoke to Him and said,

> "You will even see heaven open and the angels of
> God coming back and forth to me, the Messiah."
> (TLB)

Those angels of God were brushing around us as we all stood together, holding on to each other, praying to our dear God in His heaven — the God of peace, comfort, and love.

The angels kept together what God had brought together at that place on that particular morning. At that instant, it seemed time had stopped. We were all together with God's angels and His Holy Spirit among us. That is all we needed in this place and at this time. Praises to God, we were in the "thin place."

All of Us

I do not even understand how it all happened. It was not planned. It was not something we, as a family, had talked about. It was not something any of my siblings, our spouses, or I could take credit for. It was not something that could even be humanly possible.

You see, not all of us in our family live in the same town, and most of us work daily. Some of us have shift work, causing strange work hours. There was no date put on the calendar or plans made for all of us to visit at the same time, but we were all together on that day. What a loving, caring, considerate, gracious, and perfect God, our heavenly Father.

It was not a privilege which any of us earned or deserved, but only grace given by God. So praises to God on that Friday, when Daddy went to be with the Lord, we were all there. I believe we were all together because God wanted all of us there and allowed all of us to be there. What wonderful grace and love given to us!

I believe God wanted us together. God wanted all of Daddy's family with him, not for just the last day of his life here on this Earth — but the entire week. God put us there.

I am so thankful that my Father, God in heaven, has the

power to know all that is good for me and my family. Not only does He know all that is good for us, but He blesses us with His grace. What a real assurance to know there is no need to worry for God shows He is in control. We only need to open our spiritual eyes and see.

I have always believed, but now I share this experience to remind me that nothing has happened by coincidence or will happen by coincidence. God is in control of all things and He will take care of His people. God instructed His servant, Paul, to write in Romans 8:28,

> And we know that all that happens to us is working for our good if we love God and are fitting into his plans. (TLB)

I believe all of us needed each other, and Daddy needed his family with him. God had a plan for all of us that week — a plan for us to be together. We would be together in the "thin place." We would be together in a place with God.

It is difficult for me to find words to describe God's magnificent work. All the grand, earthly words I can think of seem too meager. All that is needed is provided from God. God provided a calmness and peace which comes only through accepting that God is in control of all things.

This peace is not a feeling provided by anything of this world. It is a peace which is only given of the Lord God and only He can provide this peace in earth or in heaven. God came to all people through Jesus Christ to show everyone His peace while He was on this earth.

On the night before Jesus Christ was arrested, and before the crucifixion, Jesus Christ washed the feet of His disciples and then talked with them as He sat with them at His last meal. Jesus told them,

> "Peace I leave with you, my peace I give unto you: not as the world giveth, give I unto you. Let not your heart be troubled, neither let it be afraid." (John 14:27 KJV)

Jesus said that himself. It is His wonderful, glorious, and gracious peace. It is the peace which God the Father and the Lord Jesus Christ provided for all of us, all together during that particular week. Not only that week, but it is the peace He offers every day.

It is astonishing and humbling to think back through the last week Daddy was awake on this earth. By grace, I was and am a witness to God's plans. God planned for a great birthday party for Daddy. Daddy may not have talked with God about a party specifically, but it seemed to be important to Daddy so it was important to God. God carried Daddy through the day. Then, on the following Friday, God received Daddy to live eternally with Him.

God really does work everything according to His will. All of this took place during the summer. The grandchildren and great-grandchildren were out of school. There would be no inconveniences of missing lessons or tests at school.

Many family members are educators. Finding a substitute for classes is a complicated process. And lesson plans must be provided. But no need to worry about finding a substitute teacher or creating lessons for the students at this time of the year.

In the summer, it was easier to focus on family and not on other concerns. What a perfect time! No one had scheduled vacations or planned events. No one was out of the state or country. Of course, we all would have made arrangements to be with Daddy if he became very sick and always had in the past. But God provided a time of convenience. God's time, as always, was perfect.

Even with the confusion that shift work can cause (or at least in my opinion) we were all able to be with Daddy.

Shift work schedules, so it seems, are set up for one to work nights for a while, days for a while, and afternoons which go into the night a while. Then the schedule provides for a long weekend off. It gets too mind boggling for me to understand.

But God understood the shift work perfectly. He provided just the right plan. God knew when the family members on shift work would have time off to be with Daddy.

Other family members worked during the day and always came by to visit just after work. Some family members were also blessed with understanding employers, knowing Daddy was very sick and allowing time off when needed.

God already had these things scheduled, but there was no way for one individual to know all of this. There was no way for one of us to keep up with all of the other siblings and their family business. But miraculously, we were all able to be together at this time.

All of the events of this last week with Daddy did not happen by accident or coincidence. We did not know what God was preparing when we made plans for the week. Thank God, He loves us enough to plan for us and guide us into His plan. It was a gracious and loving God at work!

How could it even make sense for Doug and me to drive 360 miles in one day to attend Daddy's birthday on Saturday, return home the same day, and then drive back three days later to see him again? Besides, the day before Daddy's birthday, Friday, July 4, we traveled to Florida to help entertain at a Fourth of July party with our daughter and son-in-law.

We were so glad to be asked to help. Doug and I knew we could get home from Florida on Friday and drive over to Daddy's birthday on Saturday. We somehow had no doubt in our mind. All of the traveling sounds a little insane, but there was absolutely no doubt in our minds about the trip.

As mentioned before, our son-in-law was battling cancer and this seemed to be an important event for him. He came up with an idea to have a grand cookout with his family — and what a wonderfully grand event it was. Everyone had the best time together. But that is another story of God's perfect timing and master planning. God was busy at work. Praise God, He continues planning for this family every day.

I can see now that it was God's plan. God provided all strength, safety in travel, and assurance of mind that was needed.

Remember, Doug and I made another trip to see Daddy two days after his birthday party. But, oddly enough, on this trip, we packed to stay for a while. As previously mentioned, we even packed to stay until we needed to travel on to the family reunion with Doug's family.

Even more surprising, I told Doug to pack something we might wear to a funeral. Why did I do that? It seems so strange to me even now that I was able to do this with strength, comfort, and assurance. It was like going through a process without over thinking any reason why such a thought would cross my mind.

Such a thought had never come to me before — not during any trip to the hospital or any visit during his long days of rest. I was able to pack clothes to wear to a funeral without feeling guilty, nervous, or having second thoughts —like I was being driven by another force. Never before was I willing to do such a thing. How could I ever think of such a thing?

I do not remember thinking of it as a funeral for Daddy. I just remember thinking of clothes for a funeral. But God knew we needed to stay with Mama and Daddy. He knew exactly where we needed to be.

I am thankful for a God who loves me enough to give me all the strength of mind and body that I need, in all things that I need and do. When living away from home, one may wonder if they might be home with parents when they pass away.

All I can be sure of is that God knows best and will guide as needed. God will know where everyone will need to be. Doug and I were blessed to be there in God's plan for Daddy.

It was such a surprise to all of us that Daddy agreed to bring in a hospital bed for him to sleep in. Privately, we were all a little concerned about Daddy passing away at home, in his bed with Mama. I am not sure why this thought even crossed our minds, but God took care of every detail. Again, God knew best and He still does today.

God allowed for it to be necessary for Daddy to spend only one night in a hospital bed before calling him to heaven. I believe it was God's plan for no one to be able to come together to move the furniture to fit the hospital bed until that right and perfect day. It just was not convenient on Wednesday, but Thursday was the perfect day.

It was God who provided Daddy with the mindset to agree to try using the hospital bed at that particular time. I believe, without a doubt, that God planned for Daddy to only have to spend that one night in a hospital bed. Praises to God! He is compassionate about even our small concerns.

What made the home health care nurse come by to see Daddy on Thursday night? Maybe she felt a need to see Daddy after moving him into the hospital bed. Maybe, after talking with Mama on the phone, she could hear the stress Mama was feeling — the stress of trying to give proper dosages of medication to Daddy.

Mama sometimes felt she may not have given Daddy enough medication to be comfortable, but was also concerned of giving too much medication. Again, I believe that it was no coincidence that the nurse came by at 7:00 on Thursday night to check on Daddy. This nurse was an instrument of God and fell into His plan.

The home health care nurse did not leave Mama guessing about medication dosages. No, she gave Daddy all his medication herself while she was there. Then, the nurse stayed until she knew Daddy was resting.

As mentioned, she knew how to check for signs that Daddy was resting and resting without pain. She explained these signs of rest to us. She gave us all the peace and assurance we needed as she attended to Daddy's needs. Yes, she fell right into God's plan.

How could it be that Daddy fell into a deep sleep on Sunday and Monday, two days after his birthday party, and then wake up on Tuesday to see all of us? How could it be that Daddy was able to be awake again on Wednesday and Thursday, spending time with all of us?

During those last days we had good times together, talking, laughing, singing, and praying. We enjoyed Daddy eating again with us — enjoying some of his favorite foods again.

Then, on that Friday morning, the morning Daddy did not wake, we all gathered together. I can remember getting up that morning with Doug and Mama, checking on Daddy, then getting our breakfast together while Daddy slept. Daddy had rested through the entire night, unlike the restless nights during the week. He rested in the kind of sleep that assured us that he could not be in pain.

Then I remember my siblings coming in at their own times during the morning. My sister decided to stay home from work, just in case she could help with Daddy, and my brother was already off from work that morning.

So everyone sat in the kitchen talking and visiting together while I finished cleaning the breakfast dishes. God guided each of us into His plan. God's plan was for all of us to commune with Him in the "thin place" with Daddy. What a kind, compassionate, and loving God!

Daddy always loved traveling with family, but he
enjoyed road trips even before I was born!

For if you tell others with your own mouth that
Jesus Christ is your Lord, and believe in your own
heart that God has raised him from the dead, you
will be saved. For it is believing in his heart that a
man becomes right with God; and with his mouth
he tells others of his faith, confirming his salvation.
(Romans 10:9—10 TLB)

CHAPTER

My Story

And so now I tell of the glory of God through my story. I tell it not because I have always wanted to write a story. That is something I never contemplated before. But I know God provides instruction in His Word that He should receive all praise, honor and glory. Christ Jesus instructed everyone in His Sermon on the Mount,

> "Let your light so shine before men, that they may see your good works, and glorify your Father which is in heaven." (Matthew 5:16 KJV)

God also promises to always take care of His children. I know He always does. I know He does through my experiences. I know He does by what I see. God takes care of His children even when no one realizes it at that particular moment.

Praise God for opening my spiritual eyes for me to see — to see Him and His wondrous works. I believe each person can see spiritually and graciously, if only each one will believe.

As I have mentioned, God reminded me of His wondrous work using the special scent of Daddy. It was on that particular day while cleaning house that the seed in my mind was planted to share my story.

Cleaning house sometimes turns into "thinking time" for me. My mind tends to process things while my body is busy cleaning.

I live many miles away from Mama and many months had passed since Daddy left this earth, but I smelled him very distinctly. There was a feeling of peace in the room. I even began to expect to see Daddy.

Then the wonderful ways God guided me and my family through Daddy's last week on this earth started running through my mind. It was not wonderful like a special, exciting event is wonderful, but a different kind of wonderful.

God blessed me with the ability to be there, spending Daddy's last moments with family and feeling the peace that only God can give. So I share my story in order to glorify God.

God provided the words I needed to see and understand. God sent the thoughts and words that would provide the peace and comfort needed after losing Daddy. God provides for me and speaks to me always, if I will just observe and listen.

Each day, a thought comes to my mind to help me accomplish something successfully. Or I may see something special. Then I give thanks and praise because I know my Father in His heaven is guiding me, and His Holy Spirit is with me.

Sometimes God uses others to say or do things, but I would know it was done so I would get the guidance I needed from my Heavenly Father. He is always near me. He speaks to me daily, not just on occasion, but daily.

I give Him thanks and praise for being with me always. I am someone who continuously needs guidance and does not deserve the grace I am given. But that could be another story.

His blessings and grace I claim daily. I pray daily that I may have strength to live in a way which glorifies the Lord God. Then I receive His peace. God freely provides for me, and my hope is that everyone will also receive God's graciousness and peace.

So I tell of my experiences, not just to tell another story or to tell of another real life experience. Neither is it written to merely be a short biography of Daddy. My story is intended to show the glory of my God.

I want to give Him the glory in all that I do. I give him the glory for correcting me and forgiving me in all things. All that I am which is good and right, all that I can be which is good and right, and all that I will be which is good and right is not my accomplishment, but the Lord's Spirit working in me.

In fact, most of the good things and good people in my life did not come from plans I made. My husband, my family, and my extended family are gifts from my God. So I repeat this scripture again because I cannot possibly have better words to explain the grace and love from God than these words which God gave Paul to write in Philippians so many years ago,

> Don't worry about anything: instead pray about everything; tell God your needs and don't forget to thank him for his answers. If you do this you will experience God's peace, which is far more wonderful than the human mind can understand. His peace will keep your thoughts and your hearts quiet and at rest as you trust in Christ Jesus. (Philippians 4:6–7 TLB)

God gives a peace, a peace greater than our earthly minds can even understand. Praises always to God!

So I just type. I pray these words will show the glory of God to all who will see and hear. I pray God's glory will be revealed to all who will see it and to all who will receive it. I believe that in all situations, God is good. God warns us that days on this earth may be difficult at times, but with Him, all things are possible. It is written in Matthew that Jesus Christ said,

> "Come to me and I will give you rest—all of you who work so hard beneath a heavy yoke. Wear my yoke—for it fits perfectly—and let me teach you; for I am gentle and humble, and you shall find rest for your souls; for I give you only light burdens." (Matthew 11:28—30 TLB)

The glory of God will always shine with everyone who will receive Him, and may all living beings be blessed to walk with God in the "thin place."

And yes, I miss my Daddy, but I am so happy he has peacefully returned home to God the Father. Daddy is healed, moving without pain, and wounds are gone! Daddy is enjoying the peace of our Lord Jesus Christ in the beautiful eternity He has prepared for everyone. Even when Doug and I returned to our church at home, God reassured me. God used the men's assemble to sing "Build Me Just a Cabin in the Corner of Glory Land."[1] Again, I remembered Daddy would tell us all he needed was a cabin in order to wait on his family to meet him in heaven. Praise to God! So as the last verse, of the last book, in the last chapter of The Bible states,

> The grace of our Lord Jesus Christ be with you all. Amen. (Revelation 22:21 KJV)

Amen and Amen!

Notes

Chapter 1

1   United States War Shipping Administration. <u>U.S. Maritime Service to Accept 16 Year Olds for Training</u>: PR 1889(W), May 17, 1944.

Chapter 2

1   Sammis, John H. "Trust and Obey." 1887 (Words: 1Jn 1:7).

Chapter 8

1   Garrett, Les. "This is the Day." 1967 (Words: Psalm 118:24).
2   Brumley, Albert E. "I'll Fly Away." 1929

Chapter 12

1   Monroe, Bill. "Lord Build Me a Cabin in Gloryland." 1963

My Daddy, Cecil G. McIntyre with his loving pal, Sugar.

These things I have spoken unto you, that in me ye might have peace. In the world ye shall have tribulation: but be of good cheer; I have overcome the world. (John 16:33 KJV)

I love you Daddy…

Printed in the United States
By Bookmasters